Widow Box

Carol Longenecker

Art by Monique Cronk

ISBN 978-1-64003-465-5 (Paperback)
ISBN 978-1-64003-466-2 (Digital)

Covenant Books, Inc.
11661 Hwy 707
Murrells Inlet, SC 29576
www.covenantbooks.com

To Gordon Eugene Longenecker, my husband of almost twenty-five years—born January 6, 1956, died November 8, 2005:

Christ-follower
Storyteller
Giver of second chances
Thinker
Loyal
Painter extraordinaire
Friend to everyone
Brother and son
Husband and father

Introduction

At first, I could hardly say "He died" or call myself a widow. The first time I was faced with marking the *widow* box on an application just a few months after my husband, Gordon, died, I nearly fell apart. I was unprepared. My sister-in-law told me her then three-year-old grandson called his other widowed grandmother a "window." I thought, *I can say that! I'm a window!* Yet as unprepared as I was for that and many other single moments in my journey through widowhood, I was as prepared as anyone can be for the single crisis of loss. I recently heard, "You can't prepare for a crisis in the middle of a crisis," and that was my saving grace, that I had spent years growing my spiritual roots deep into God's Word. Here is Gordon's story and my story, followed by God's story, helping it all make as much sense as it possibly can.

My Story

My walk into widowhood began on a Sunday night, November 6, 2005, with the words "Gordon's missing." I was driving home alone from a four-day trip, seeing our children in college, when my ringing cell phone interrupted my happy thoughts with those words that were to change my life and challenge my faith.

The night before I left on my trip, we had had a nice Wednesday evening furniture shopping together. Then Thursday morning, Gordon got up early to head off to work. I got up to prepare for my trip, plus making his favorite potato soup to leave with him before heading to Missoula, Montana, where our daughter, Megan, was in grad school. Gordon was planning a one-day hunting trip for Saturday with a buddy, Paul, and I would return Sunday evening. Saturday night, I phoned him as I

5

stood outside under a snowy nighttime sky and learned that he had postponed his hunting until the next day. Sunday afternoon, I left Missoula to stop in Bozeman, Montana, where our son, Brian, was in Bible College to have dinner with him before the last two-hour drive to Billings. I had had a glorious four days.

As I neared Billings and was able to pick up one of the Christian radio stations, I turned the volume up quite loud to be heard over the hum of the tires on the highway in the dark winter night. Suddenly, just a half hour from Billings, I realized my cell phone was ringing on the seat beside me. I turned the radio down to hear from one of Gordon's buddies, Tim, who wasn't hunting with him, telling me, "Gordon's missing." In disbelief, I stopped on the shoulder, asking, "What do you mean?" Hunting buddy Paul was running out of battery on his cell phone and didn't have my cell number, so he had called his sister to locate Tim to see if his wife had my cell number. In my stunned state, I asked what I should do and where Gordon was missing, wondering if I should drive to the vicinity. Tim told me to go home and wait until daylight, then ride with him to the search site, a place neither of us had ever been. Paul had told Tim that a search team was assembling but couldn't really do anything until daylight.

If I thought *that* was the longest night of my life, the next one was going to be even longer. As I lay on top of my bed in my clothes, I could not sleep. Not knowing what kind of place Gordon was in, I didn't even know how to imagine anything. I was scared, but he had to be even more scared. I was not prepared for such news, but I could only hope that he was "hunter prepared." My mind went over what I needed to take with me in the morning when I had no idea where we were going. Fortunately, I grabbed long underwear and snow boots; both of which were needed.

Gordon's Story

Gordon loved telling stories, especially hunting stories, and he was good at it, but he was about to leave the last one for *me* to tell. He and buddy Paul had headed up the Bridger Creek Road off I-90 between Reed Point and Big Timber, Montana, early in the morning. Gordon had long wanted to see what was at the end of the Bridger Creek Road in the Absaroka foothills ever since we had gone Christmas tree "hunting" there many years earlier nearer the interstate. They had all the right weather gear for early November in Montana, plus a handgun and rifles, two-way radios, and a GPS. The outcome hinged on what Gordon didn't have, what he didn't do, what didn't work, and the uncooperative weather. What he didn't have was his thermal blanket in his fanny pack.

What he didn't do was sit and wait when he knew he was lost. What didn't work was the two-way radio from right after he walked into the trees. And the weather turned to overcast with snow, and then a heavy fog set in.

Gordon and Paul had no hunting luck all day, but not surprisingly, Gordon wanted to make one last attempt at the very last half hour of daylight for what should have been a short twenty-minute cut across a forested slope. The weather had been pleasant enough that Gordon had taken off the warmer layer of his coat and exchanged his hiking boots for his tennis shoes before taking off for one last hope for a deer. While none of that was wise, it is what he did.

Because Paul had bad knees, he would be the one to drop Gordon off at the top side of the hill and pick him up at the bottom ... only Gordon never came out of the trees, and it got dark, and the temperatures dropped. Paul drove back and forth on the narrow dirt road, honking his horn between the drop off point and the pickup point, fear mounting. Finally, he knew he had to call 911 for help to the Sweet Grass County Sheriff's Department, and with his battery running low, he needed to let me know Gordon was missing.

My Story

Although it wasn't yet daylight, I couldn't wait any longer in my house, so I drove to Tim's to sit outside to wait for him to get up and ready to drive to the search site. I was numb in my thoughts. I couldn't believe this was happening to us! Tim and I drove in mostly silence, lost in our imaginations of what lay ahead. I had called my children, my mother, Gordon's sister and his parents, and my dearest friend Sharon. Sharon said, "Perhaps God wants some time alone with Gordon," and I found such comfort in those words, taking God up on them. Word spread, but I was oblivious. People were praying all across the nation for a good outcome, but I was unaware.

By the time we finally found the search site, a search team from the Sweet Grass County Sheriff's Department had assembled.

We were so remote and tucked down and away that to receive any cell service we had to drive to a higher point. There was some snow on the ground, and it was overcast and snowing lightly with temperatures around thirty degrees. My brother Brian arrived with my mother, but we were in the wilds, and there were no restrooms nor any food, and they could not stay very long. I was wishing Gordon could see the team of people assembled when I realized Brian had a camera on his seat. I felt embarrassed that I wanted to document the scene for Gordon and our children, but I decided that if I didn't do so, I would wish I had. So camera in hand, I snapped five pictures that I treasure to this day.

It was cold outside, so sometimes I sat in one person or another's vehicle with the heater on, or I stood outside alongside the searchers and friends. No one had thought about food, but I found Oreos and granola bars in one of the pickups. I had not eaten since the night before, but my sense of hunger was eclipsed by worry and fear.

The searchers had maps spread out on the hood of one of the pickups, strategizing about where to go. Gordon and Paul also had a map and knew how to read it, and Gordon was carrying a compass, which he knew how to use, but as the searchers compared Paul's map with their map, it became apparent that Paul's was a bit off. There was no room for error in finding the point that Gordon was to meet up with Paul. The pine trees were so thick and the terrain so hilly that you could be only yards away from a trail and not even know it. We know Gordon came pretty close to the end of that road, but he couldn't see it.

A call was put in to the Absaroka search dog team, but they weren't able to arrive until early afternoon. A call was also put in to Malmstrom Air Force Base in Great Falls for a plane to fly over the search area, but it was too overcast to be safe or effective. Tim thought the search area needed to be expanded to include the area Gordon was eventually found, but the lead didn't agree, so it was not expanded.

The search dog team arrived and began debriefing on the situation. As they prepared their gear and the dog, they asked me important questions: How fit is Gordon? What did he have with him, and what was he wearing? Would he shoot a dog that looks like a wolf if he saw it? How does he handle stressful situations? And the biggie … Will he walk or will he wait if he knows he is lost? Those of us who knew Gordon weighed in with our answers:

He is fairly fit. He had a rifle and a handgun, a GPS, and a two-way radio and was wearing a fanny pack, but we didn't know what was in it. He had only one layer of his coat on and was wearing tennis shoes instead of his boots because, after all, this was only supposed to be a twenty-minute hike under pleasant conditions. He handles stress fairly well, and he knows all the rules of hunting safety, but *will he walk, or will he wait?*

For that answer, I went back two years when he and Paul were on an overnight hunting trip but in hilly, treeless terrain. It was the end of daylight, but they could not find their truck in the darkness. They could find their camper, which was in a different location, but the truck contained their cell phones to call me and tell me they wouldn't be home that night, so I wouldn't worry. Gordon knew if he didn't get a hold of me, I would call the sheriff, so there was only one thing to do—start walking to the nearest ranch house, which ended up being ten miles away. Paul's knees were not able to carry him the whole way, so Gordon gave him the thermal blanket out of his own fanny pack and left Paul to sit and wait for help. Gordon never replaced that thermal blanket in his fanny pack. It could have been a lifesaver two years later if he had done so. Gordon arrived at the ranch house at midnight, where he knocked on their door and used their phone to call me. By then, I was frantic and had been contemplating at what point I should alert the sheriff.

Because of this experience I *knew* that Gordon would walk rather than wait because he would think he better get himself out of this mess so I wouldn't panic. Against all his training, he did walk.

Waiting! That is all I could do. I could not be a part of the search team as I was neither skilled nor prepared and the terrain was rough. Wondering! Is he just injured, or had he had a heart attack and he is waiting for us to find him? Praying! For Gordon as he waits to be found. For Gordon as he thinks about his family and what this is doing to them. For Gordon as he is having a lot of alone time with God.

It may seem crazy, but it never occurred to me that Gordon could be lost! He always knew where he was with his uncanny sense of direction, whether in a big city with unfamiliar landmarks or the wilds with his compass. Even as the hours slowly passed, I only thought of him as injured, not *lost*.

It was nearing the end of winter daylight, and I had neither eaten nor slept for nearly twenty-four hours. Some of Gordon's friends who had shown up throughout the day had had to return to Billings, but Collin arrived to stay as long as it took to find Gordon. His wife, Patty, made the trip later in the day to bring him warmer clothes for the cold night. My brother Brian told me I needed to go with Patty back into Big Timber to eat and find a motel (perhaps a forty-five-minute drive). I complied, but before I left we learned the search dog had picked up Gordon's scent, and hope rose. It could still be hours because the terrain was rugged and there was snow and it was dark.

Around 5:00 p.m. someone drove me into Big Timber to meet up with my friend Patty. We met at the sheriff's office and told them where they could call us when they had news. After picking at my food in a restaurant, we took a room in a motel and turned on the news to hear about a missing hunter, my husband. Exhausted, I crawled into bed, but the phone rang soon after 10:00 p.m., and Patty, whether accurately or inaccurately, heard that Gordon had been found, and he was only slightly hypothermic, and they would begin bringing him into town. We were only in our room for an hour when we checked out to sit out the rest of the night in the sheriff's office, though we had no idea at the time that it really would be the rest of the night.

As time slowly passed, we heard the two-way radio chatter about Gordon and quickly realized things were worse than we had thought. He was severely hypothermic, and it was a long, tedious drive over rough and rutted roads to bring him to where a helicopter could pick him up. First, he was loaded onto an ATV to take him about a mile to the waiting ambulance for the drive out of the mountains. With a severely hypothermic person, they had to drive extremely slow to not jar his heart. About 3:00 a.m. I looked outside to see an eerie, thick fog that we would soon learn would prevent the helicopter from arriving. Patty and I sat on hard wooden chairs such as you would find in an old auditorium where the seats tip up. I leaned my head back, but sleep was impossible, and I had been awake for about thirty hours. It was a surreal situation.

About 4:30 a.m. we heard that a helicopter had been dispatched to meet at the intersection of Bridger Creek Road and Interstate 90, so we jumped in Patty's car to drive the fifteen miles there in the fog. In addition to the fog, it was still dark, and we couldn't see anything but some headlights off the highway, which we realized was the ambulance headed into Big Timber, and no helicopter was in sight. We heard from the sheriff that the ambulance was headed to the little airport for transport, so I told Patty, "Let's turn around again and head back to Billings [sixty-five miles] because as soon as they load him they will fly to Billings and be there before we can."

It was about 6:00 a.m. when we arrived at the hospital. I had alerted my friend Sharon to be there, and she called the others and my pastor to join us. They were more aware than I was that the news would not be good because they had been given a private waiting room. I still held on to a shred of hope for Gordon as the doctor came into the room and, sitting down in front of me, told me Gordon had died. A shock like I had never known flowed through my arms. I asked to see him and then was shocked again when he said that Gordon wasn't there. I asked, just as Mary did about Jesus's body, "What do you mean he's not here?" Because Gordon died in another county, they couldn't bring his body to Billings until the coroner there gave his permission, perhaps twenty-four hours. I was now a widow. I didn't know how to tell my children, Megan and Brian.

Sharon took me home, and the sleep I so desperately needed I did not want. Friends took over my kitchen as my children and Gordon's sister and parents arrived from out of town and out of state. I did not know how to plan a funeral, but with their help, we did, and it was glorious! God was in it and all around us! He was in the details as well as the bigger picture.

God's Story

This is not just Gordon's story or my story; it is God's story! It would be even sadder if that were not so! Hunting partner Paul said, "God let Gordon's foibles play out to this end." I have always quoted, "God is never early and never late," and now was the biggest test of whether I really believed it. God could have had Gordon keep his hiking boots on and put on his other layer of coat. He could have kept the clouds, fog, and snow at bay. He could have had Gordon put another thermal blanket in his fanny pack or let the fire start in spite of the wet wood. He could have kept Gordon from walking rather than waiting for help or from going out at nearly the end of daylight for one last attempt at a deer. He could have led Gordon to the right place to meet up with Paul. He *could* have! God wasn't late for Gordon. In fact

He was right *with* Gordon through the whole ordeal. I never was angry at God, nor even Gordon and his foibles.

I immersed myself in the Psalms after the funeral, reading slowly to personalize meaningful passages. As the weeks passed, other passages gave me *comfort*. As I read scripture, I felt wrapped in a warm blanket of security in the God who knows me and loves me. "Surely God is my help, the Lord is the one who sustains me" (Psalm 54:4) became my answer to how I was doing in the months following. Not only was He sustaining me, but He was giving me joy! "Bring joy to your servant for to you, O Lord, I lift up my soul" (Psalm 86:4). I was unprepared for the ability to know both sorrow and joy in the same moment! "Though the fig tree does not bud and there are no grapes on the vines, though the olive crop fails and the fields produce no food, though there are no sheep in the pen and not cattle in the stalls, YET I will rejoice in the Lord, I will be joyful in God my Savior. The Sovereign Lord is my strength; he makes my feet like the feet of a deer, he enables me to go on the heights" (Habakkuk 3:17–19).

Yes, it was God *enabling* me to go on! "Put your hope in God, for I will YET praise Him, my Savior and my God" (Psalm 42:5 and 11). I was grounded in scripture, and scripture was grounding me in my grief.

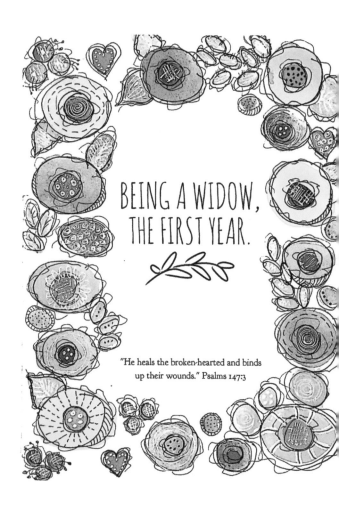

BEING A WIDOW, THE FIRST YEAR.

"He heals the broken-hearted and binds up their wounds." Psalms 147:3

A Widow

The loss of my husband of nearly twenty-five years left a gaping hole. I was only fifty-two. The unfinished book *The Excellent Wife* (by Martha Peace) sat with a marker frozen in place between its pages. There is no longer an urgency to pick it up again. Photo albums will no longer be of a family of four, but completed scrapbooks softened the edges of that jagged hole. My then twenty-three-year-old daughter asked, "Who will walk me down the aisle?" And I wonder how I will be able to support myself, take care of the yard, live alone. Who do I call about adjusting the automatic thermostat, the broken shower door, or with computer or car repair questions? Who will finish the projects he started? With whom will I reminisce about the trip to Georgia and Alabama when it was just the two of us to remember?

Gordon won't be there to share our dreams for the future or sit with me in church or fall asleep on my couch. I won't have a reason to fix his favorite potato soup or pecan pie. There are so many layers to losing a husband that only time would reveal—and often unexpectedly. I never thought "till death do us part" would come so young and in this way.

I learned that grief is like a shadow—a permanent, attached part of me. It used to cast a long, obvious shadow, but now, even though that shadow is short and sometimes hidden, it is and always will be there. I have learned that you cannot fully understand grief's broken heart until you experience it yourself. I learned that sorrow and joy can exist side by side, not only in the same day but in the same moment. I learned that my anchor in Christ was strong enough to hold me through the storm. I learned that I needed salty tears to wash my broken heart. I learned that just as others' lives continued on around me, I had to make my own also go on. I learned how to redefine "a hope and a future" because my future was no longer linked to my spouse. I am learning to deal with loneliness as I learn to fill the holes left by my husband's death. I learned that grief is weird, making me feel conspicuous yet invisible, surrounded yet alone, comforted yet afraid. I learned to do the things I think I cannot do. I learned that every loss has layers. I learned how to navigate through my own journey of loss and pain. My belief that God is never early and never late was tested to the max, and I came through the experience with that belief still intact. Above all, I can say with the Psalmist that "I have seen the goodness of the Lord in the land of the living" (Psalm 27:13).

Loss of Identity

It doesn't take long before you realize you have lost a big part of your identity. You don't know where you fit in any more. Are you married or single? Because you still feel married. It was such a part of your life that you wore it like an identity. My "with" person is gone! I might be beside someone, but my "with" person is not there. When I would go out alone on a Saturday night and someone I know would see me, they would ask, "Who are you with?" "No one," I reply, and I ache inside. My "with" person still walks beside me invisibly as I still imagine him there. *With* is such a simple word, totally unnoticed before I was a widow, yet now it brings up pain. *With*—used as a function word to indicate combination, accompaniment, presence or addition. Now my "with" person is Jesus, the ultimate *with*. Comfort comes when I acknowledge Jesus is *with* me. He is the "with" person who softens the jagged edge left by the one I am without.

The Wedding Ring

A year after Gordon died, a friend who had been a widow for a few years asked me what I thought I would do about wearing my ring. I was not prepared when she asked me, "Do you think of yourself as married?" and I did not have an answer for her or for myself. I was not ready to just take my ring off, but I was ready to ponder her question. I did and do feel I identify more with married people than never-married people, but that still didn't address the question of "did I think of myself as married." I had to separate that I *felt* married from that I *wasn't* married to free myself to replace the ring with something else meaningful. The options I saw were to create a new piece of jewelry with that ring or to consider something like a friendship or birthstone ring. As I was shopping, none of those options appealed to me. Then I found a dainty Yogo sapphire ring that was meaningful because Gordon had lived where many Yogos are mined in Montana. When I found the right ring, I found my answer! And I wear it on my right hand. There is no rule nor right answer nor a timetable for *you*.

New Normal: Creating a New Rhythm

Grief is very physical, and you will be exhausted. As much as you need extra sleep, do not stay in bed all morning. When you first wake up, *get* up and *get* dressed. Even if you do not have any place to go nor plan to see anyone, do those two things. Then make your bed so you will not be tempted to get back in it. Eat! You must eat regularly, which, if you are now alone, will be much harder because no one sees if you do or don't or whether you are making healthy choices. At first, I would sit alone at the table because that's what *we* did. Then a couple years later, I allowed myself to eat at the counter. After a couple more years, I gave myself permission to set up a TV tray in the living room, and now I just fix a plate to hold on my lap in front of the TV. While my eating place changed, I made sure my cooking did not suffer. Seek out the things that can bring you joy, whether they be spending time with grand-children or coffee dates with friends. *You* may have to be the initiator because others might not know if it is okay to call you.

Loneliness

This is inevitable! One *Webster* definition is "sad from being alone." You no longer have your "with" person, so you can feel lonely even in a group who cares about you. Over time, you will have to become okay with being alone, which doesn't have to mean you like it. You have to not expect others to fill the gap of your "with" person and give yourself permission to sit alone in a restaurant or church or go to a concert or movie alone. The first times were not easy, but it was more effort to try to find someone who would go with me. Loneliness has been my biggest hurdle, but it has also been my greatest growth in confidence that I am okay even when I am alone.

Major Decisions and Firsts

Plenty has been written about not making any major decisions in the first year, so I won't elaborate. Those decisions can be as big as selling your house or even dating (yes, that sounds weird now) or as small as removing your ring or rearranging your furniture. In one year, things will *look* different even though they may not actually *be* different! Emptying the closet and drawers of your "with" person's clothes can happen any time in the first year that you are comfortable with it. Not that that has to be done in the first year, but it is in that year that you begin to think about it. You may want to do that alone as I did, or enlist the help of a dear friend or family member. Then there are all the *firsts*: their birthday or even your birthday without them, Christmas, Thanksgiving, anniversary, even Valentine's Day, when others celebrate their loved ones. Now you have a new date to remember: the day they died. What would you like to do when *that* date arrives at the end of your first year? It's not a date to celebrate but rather a date to *remember* or to *acknowledge.* I chose to schedule a massage around that date each year. You live with their absence *every* day, not just on special days. Your sorrow knows no specific date, but it feels good, and it is honoring to acknowledge their absence.

Tears

This was a relatively new emotion for me, but now I was daily feeling the saltiness and coolness of tears slowly rolling down my cheeks. Sometimes the tears are quiet as they seep out in quiet remembering, and sometimes they are loud with audible sobs of loud remembering. They remind me I have lost someone. They are a release and relief, and they actually comfort me. For a long time, I was almost afraid for them to stop altogether because I was afraid that would mean I was forgetting Gordon. Tears are about remembering! I became not ashamed to cry in front of people though sometimes I would hold back for *their* comfort. If you cannot find time to be alone with your tears because of children and a full-time job, you need to give yourself permission to find a time and place to not hold them back. I believe tears are an important and honest expression of our loss that we need not keep hidden from others. In the Psalms, David wrote, "You keep track of all my sorrows. You have collected all my tears in your bottle. You have recorded each one in your book" (56:8). They are precious to God!

Sacred Spaces, Sacred Things

One of the layers you have to deal with is their spaces and their things. Spaces can be the chair they always sat on in the living room or the dining room. It can be their side of the garage or their side of the bed. Spaces now empty yet we still allow them to remain empty. It feels odd for *us* to sit there, park there, or lie there. It's like it's a sacred space, *their* space. Gordon and I had our usual sides of the bed, but when he died, it took more than a year to give my legs permission to spread out a little. Even in a motel, we had "sides" of the bed. I didn't think it mattered in a motel, but it did to Gordon! Sacred things can be their work shoes, their dresser top, the book they were reading ... the normal things you don't want to disturb

39

because they make you feel like they are going to come back to use them again soon. Grieve those spaces and those things because they are a part of remembering. Don't rush to fill them or move them. I left Gordon's work shoes in the same space outside the closet for many years because it comforted me.

Ask!

It is hard for most women to ask for help. My biggest ongoing needs were for computer help and yard advice. Ask yourself, who do you know and who did your husband know that could help with this? When it came to my yard, Gordon would have conversations with my best friend and a neighbor man, so I asked them twice a year to both come over and walk through my yard with me and tell me what to be doing. When it came to computer questions, I found a girlfriend who was willing to help me. One time, my small group came over and helped me repaint my deck, and another time, a few women came to help me spread weed mat and new bark in my shrubs. A neighboring husband has helped with some basic plumbing needs. Another husband fixed my doorbell. All these people were willing, but none of them would have known what I needed if I didn't ask. I am careful to not use one man for all my needs and make sure I have a good relationship with his wife to avoid any opportunity for gossip or scandal. In the ideal world, our church would check with us every few months to ask what we needed help with, but that is unrealistic in most cases. Sometimes all you need is an opinion and someone to bounce thoughts off. Please ask for help!

Dream Again

Perhaps you and your husband were so caught up in work and home that you hadn't taken time to dream together. Perhaps you had put your own dreams on hold while you raised a family. Perhaps you couldn't even identify one from your past or present. When I read in Jeremiah 29:11, "'For I know the plans I have for you,' declares the Lord, 'plans to give you hope and a future,'" I could accept hope, but I could not see a future. I could not dream. Gordon and I had talked for over a year about driving up to Banff in Alberta, Canada, but the trip never materialized. In my second year of being a widow, I talked with my daughter about losing my future and about our hope to drive to Banff. I was shocked when she said, "We can do that!" I said "We? Who is we? Like you, me, and Brian?" And she said "Yes!" I cannot tell you how much that lifted me and set me on a journey of dreaming! I told her, "Even if we never go, I am getting so much mileage out of the fact that we *could* go!" Perhaps your dream is a hobby you had let go or a volunteer opportunity that has tugged at your heart that you never had time for. It could be a trip you had hoped to take together or a kitchen remodel you had talked about. It is powerful to have something to look forward to! Dreams don't come knocking at your door; they are up to you to imagine. Ask God to help you dream again!

Journal the Journey

This is not an assignment, just a suggestion. It is not about punctuation or sentence structure. It doesn't have to even be done daily. But there is such therapy in writing down the emotions and events of your grief journey that even if no one else ever reads it, *you* will have benefited. You may think you will always remember things, but time has a way of making fuzzy even the most memorable events of our lives. Most important is the recording of God's presence in our circumstance as we pour out the raw emotion of our hearts on paper to Him. He already knows our thoughts anyway! It's not too late to start, even if it has been months since you became a widow. And it doesn't have to be a fancy journal. Even a simple spiral notebook will do.

It's Time to Move On

What does that really mean? Do people say it because our grief makes them uncomfortable? Or are you actually not seeing something in yourself they see in you that worries them? Find your "safe people" that you can talk about your husband with even long past the point that you should have "moved on." Give that person or persons permission to tell you if they are worried and then listen to them. But ultimately, only *you* can measure if you are "moving on" as you look back on your journey thus far. Only *you* can decide what "moving on" actually looks like for you. "Moving on" is *not* leaving your memories behind, nor does it mean not talking about the spouse ever again. Perhaps you prefer the words "moving forward" because they don't imply you are leaving your past behind. You just cannot leave your past behind! Remember that you can no more detach a shadow from yourself on a sunny day than you can detach grief and memories from you ever. Grief will always be there as the shadow is, just not always obvious. Perhaps that is what "moving on" really is—when others can't see the shadow of our grief unless we show it to them by stepping into the sunshine. Trust yourself on this one!

Isaiah 61:2-3

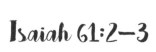

This is "the year of the Lord's favor ... to comfort all who mourn and provide for those who grieve in Zion—to bestow on them a crown of beauty instead of ashes, the oil of gladness instead of mourning, and a garment of praise instead of a spirit of despair. [You] will be called oaks of righteousness, a planting of the Lord for the display of his splendor." This is what God wants to give you when you give Him your mourning and your despair!

The Second Year

As you move into your second year, you may find yourself torn between feeling happy to have some distance from your initial intense grief and knowing that same distance is taking you further from your husband. I found that I wanted to hang on to the deep closeness to God I had in those first months even though it came out of pain. I felt sadness over feeling I was drifting away from my intense closeness to God born out of sorrow and drifting away from the feeling of my husband's presence. I wrestled with this in my second year as I sought to find balance between them, even feeling some guilt over the struggle that I wouldn't have known the closeness if I hadn't known the loss. The passing of time and the lessening of the pain is inevitable, but moving forward is optional. For most, this year is more difficult as the loss becomes more reality. He really is gone. He really is not coming back. I chose to remember and celebrate what we had been as a couple while I discovered who I am alone. I have found I am more capable than I ever thought I could be!

Prayer

"God, help me accept the fact that my life has forever changed and that my future will be different in ways that are as yet invisible. Help me let that future unfold under Your direction. Help me not rush the grief process as it impacts the rest of my life. Help me realize that You want to be my resource even when You seem absent, silent, or far away. I acknowledge that my husband's death did not take you by surprise, and thank You that You are a 'defender of widows' (Psalm 68:5b). Help me with any unforgiveness associated with my loss, and help me know how to grieve healthily. I want to be called an oak of righteousness, a planting of the Lord for the display of Your splendor."

If you have read this far and realize you do not know God to know His comfort, now may be the time for you to ask Jesus to take over the leadership of your life. Tell Him you are sorry for any sin in all your past because He is waiting to give you His white robes of righteousness to wear in place of your rags of sin. Accept His promise of a new creation because you are now born again. Begin today to learn about Him from His written Word by reading a Psalm a day alongside one of the gospels (suggested if you are new to the Bible). Welcome to God's family!

Epilogue

It has been more than ten years since I became a widow without remarrying. You may say it's one thing to write about the first year or even the second year, but what about the third, the fifth, the tenth? How have I changed or not changed? I had read about how to manage grief but not how to manage life as a widow. I could never have imagined ten years of being alone, of letting go of dreams and finding new ones, of managing my yard and my finances, and of grandchildren not knowing their grampa Gordon.

I have a confidant, a long-time dear friend, to whom I can tell anything and who never, to this day, minds the tears that still occasionally come. I truly thank God for her and do not know where I would be without her listening ear and her prayers for me and my children. I hope you have found or will find such a person in your life. I hope you will be that person to someone else because of your experience of loss.

I still journal whenever God impresses something on me or I am in an interesting circumstance. If it's something reflecting on Gordon, I mark it with a red heart. Someday my children and grandchildren will find new insights into my thoughts as they read what I found important. If I were to save anything from my house if there were a fire, it would be my journals and pictures!

My adult children, who were twenty and twenty-two when they lost their dad, have married and given me five grandsons. We talk about their dad often and the little boys know about grampa Gordon. Right after he died, my daughter sobbed. "Who will walk me down the aisle?" My heart broke for her. The answer came five years later when her brother had that honor. They both are walking with the Lord.

Finances are one area that I have seen God's faithfulness to me. My journal charts the hills and valleys of my financial journey—

when I have been uncertain and when I have been surprised, when I have had barely enough and when I had an abundance. I never had to have a full- or part-time job while married, but there have been times that that has been necessary after the direct-sales company I was with decided to close its doors. Gratefully, I have remained debt-free.

But finances are second to being alone. I learned that I needed to be around people even if they are strangers. In talking to other widows, I have found that most struggle with weekends alone. For me, it is still Saturday evenings, so I try to seek out someone to do something rather than my all-too-often companion of TV. If no one is available, I will go alone to a coffee shop buzzing with activity. I think I took for granted the companionship of marriage until it was taken from me.

I could not imagine that I would be alone for more than ten years. I miss Gordon in some way literally every single day, though not usually with tears. He floats in and out of my thoughts because he is still a part of me. I have tried online dating services but with very limited success. I don't want aloneness to be the driving force behind dating and remarriage. I know that the adjustment to being married again in my sixties would be greater than in my twenties. I would rather be alone than with the wrong person! And I am grateful for God using my aloneness to share with other widows as an encouragement. I know that if I remarry, I will be less available because I won't have just myself to think of. Some women love the freedom of being alone, not having to check in with anyone or cook for them, and admittedly, that is nice, but only to a point.

Spiritually, I have grown deeper in my relationship and reliance on God. I see scripture through the lens of my experience, and it is richer for it. I think back to the first months when I immersed myself in the Psalms and how I poured out my heart in tears to God. Though that time was unbelievably painful, it was unexplainably sweet as God became my comforter. Today, as in 2005, my favorite verse to live by is Proverbs 3:5 and 6: "Trust in the Lord with all your heart and lean not on your own understanding; in all your ways acknowledge him and he will make your paths straight." It is easy to become fearful or anxious in my aloneness, but Philippians 4:6 and 7 also remind me to "not be anxious about anything, but in everything by prayer and petition, with thanksgiving, present your [my] requests to God. And the peace of God which transcends all understanding will guard your [my] hearts and your minds in Christ Jesus."

The single hardest thing so far, other than being the only parent at my children's weddings, was the sale of my house in my tenth year after twenty-two years of living in it. The big yard was getting beyond my control, and the exterior was starting to need repair, requiring money I didn't have. I gave myself a year to wrap my mind and emotions around what I knew I needed to do. I set a goal of six months to sort through every nook and cranny, closets and boxes, and set a garage sale date followed by a listing date. It was a daunting process to go through alone! The house sold in three days, and I kicked into high gear to close in two months. I had to leave my emotions at the front door as I packed up my life. But at my final goodbye,

I sobbed through prayer for all the memories we made there and the ones the new family would make within those walls. I had met with them and told them about Gordon, the condition of the fixer-upper the house was when we bought it and all the things he did to it, and their appreciation gave me closure. I didn't lose the memories we made nor the possessions that filled those walls; I was losing seeing all the things Gordon did to improve the house and yard. I felt like I was leaving a big piece of Gordon behind! I closed the door literally and figuratively on that chapter and walked into a new one with no regret.

I still find myself toying with my ringless finger, thinking of Gordon when I think of his favorite foods, wishing we were shopping for a trailer together and mowing the lawn at a diagonal because that's what he did. I still can't believe I'm a widow and that I'm managing my finances alone. At the ten-year mark, I wrote in my journal:

Ten years ago tragedy walked in the door UNinvited. It set down its bags of grief and sorrow in the living room for thirty hours then unpacked them. It moved in and spread into every nook and cranny.

BUT ... God walked into the door of my house INvited. He immediately unpacked His bags of hope and joy and spread them over tragedy into every nook and cranny.

Tragedy never leaves, BUT neither does God.

That is where you will find me today— ever missing Gordon, ever trusting God.

> Wishing you a faith journey,
> Carol Longenecker

Resources

Cowman, L. B. *Streams in the Desert.*

Griefshare, a thirteen-week faith-based program with a video and workbook.

Sittser, Jerry. *A Grace Disguised.*

Wright, Norman. *Experiencing Grief.*

About the Author

Carol Longenecker is a native Montanan with two children and six grandchildren. She likes trips to New Zealand, Bible study, reading, coffee dates, summer concerts in the park, and scrapbooking. She is so grateful for every album with photos of her husband, Gordon, that she was able to display at his funeral.

CPSIA information can be obtained
at www.ICGtesting.com
Printed in the USA
LVHW072008250122
709353LV00010B/358